The Foot Brothers

The Foot Brothers

Arthur Jude with Dick Hoy

© 2017 Arthur Jude with Dick Hoy
All rights reserved.

ISBN: 1479342041
ISBN 13: 9781479342044

Chapter 1

Fall leaves crunched under their feet as the brothers hotfooted it to Grandpa's house. It was the perfect night for coon hunting, with coonskins bringing about fifteen dollars per pelt. This kind of money could last the boys all school year, or at least through Christmas. Art, being the oldest, was the only one permitted to carry the gun and to shoot it. Dick carried the bullets, a little bit like Barney Fife. Their mother made the rule long ago. Dick also was in charge of Grandpa's coonhound, Frosty.

Dodging the mudholes and ruts along the road, Dick noticed just how big Art's footprints were. Art had been wearing Dad's rubber boots for some time now. Dick could not help laughing about just how big they really were. Art had been self-conscious about his size since his growth spurt, but Dick could not stop laughing, calling him everything from T-Rex to Elephant Man. Dick mentioned that someday, three or four million years from now, when geologists finds Art's footprints in the mud, they will wonder what kind of monster it was.

When Dick finally settled on Bigfoot, the fight was on. It was not much of a fight, Art grabbing Dick by the shirt collar with both hands and lifting him off the ground. Of course, Dick's fists were flailing away when

Arthur Jude with Dick Hoy

Art noticed Dick's footprints in the mud. They were so much smaller than his. Art started laughing at just how much smaller Dick's footprints were and making some crude remarks about his private parts, and he turned Dick loose. Dick hit the ground with enough time for one more punch.

Everything being OK now, they continued their trip. "You know," said Art, "at least you are not a chicken. That's why, from now on, my secret name for you will be Chicken. Chicken Foot, that is."

"Oh yeah?" retorted Dick. "From now on, my secret name for you is Bigfoot." Both boys realized they had something that would last a lifetime.

Off in the distance, Frosty, Grandpa's old coonhound, began howling, alert to the boys on their way for a great night of coon hunting as they turned into the gravel lane that led to Grandpa's house. Frosty really cut loose in his eagerness to go hunting as well. Dick went to pet Frosty as Art went in to see Grandpa and Grandma.

Grandpa was sitting in his rocking chair, watching the evening news with Walter Cronkite. Grandma was in the kitchen, cleaning up the evening dishes. Aunt Sharon was running around the house, getting ready for her Friday night date with Billy Bob. She thought maybe tonight he would ask the big question, and she was in a tizzy.

Their home was not a mansion, but it was really good to live in. The Warm Morning stove was banked way down, so it could be flared up early in the morning to take the chill out of the house. Grandpa had already brought in the coal for the next day. The coal bucket was a perfect place for Art to sit on, as it was close to Grandpa, and he could watch Walter Cronkite as well. Also, he wanted to show Grandpa his new trick binoculars, the kind that left a black ring around the user's eyes. Dick finally came in and gathered up some table scraps that Grandma had set aside and went right back out the door to give them to Frosty. Grandma had instructed Dick to bring the plate right back so she could wash it. Returning the plate, Dick went immediately to Grandpa's lap and wiggled a comfortable place to rest.

The Foot Brothers

All three became interested in the evening news; even Grandma stuck her head in to see what Walter was talking about. Aliens. The news was full of it. People in California were being abducted. Some of them were volunteering to take rides on the spaceships; others had formed clubs, waiting in line for their chance to meet these people from other worlds. Those who had been abducted were being interviewed. What fantastic stories they were telling! The planets they visited, the creatures they had seen and talked to. What a wonderful life we all could expect when they come and take over the Earth. Some of the women even said these space travelers impregnated them. Sharon, still in her tizzy, and Grandma too, both confirmed that aliens could be coming here.

Grandpa could not take it anymore. They had never seen him laugh so hard. Dick came rolling off his lap, tears running down Grandpa's face from laughing so hard. Grandpa had to put his foot down. "There will never be any aliens coming to this Earth!" Both women seemed to settle down after that.

Art was still sitting on the coal bucket, watching Walter through his binoculars. Without really touching his eyes, he would switch ends with them. Sometimes Walter was as close as Grandpa; other times, he was as far away as the space travelers. He did notice that the black ring material did not come off on his hands or fingers very easily. So he spit on his finger and rubbed some coal dust onto the ring of the binoculars. The next person who looked through them was going to get the full effect.

Outside in the distance, they all could hear Billy Bob's brand-new 1957 Ford Crown Victoria coming down the lane. Man, what a sharp car. He had Glass-Pack mufflers installed, so it really sounded nice. Also, he had the horn replaced with the southern rabble rat-a-to-to. Billy had graduated high school a year ago and was lucky enough to land a good job at the Kyger Creek power plant. Most other jobs here in southern Ohio were strip mines or county work, with some people working on the Ohio River barge traffic.

The boys did not know just how good it was growing up in southern Ohio.

You'd think Sharon was going to pee her undies with the sounds of Billy Bob coming down the lane. She was taking some time to gather herself, asking Grandma what she looked like. "You look good. Do you think he is really going to ask you tonight?" asked Grandma.

Sometimes Sharon and Billy Bob would take Art and Dick with them to the Kanawn Drive-In and then to the Bob Evans drive-in for strawberry pie. Boy, what a treat, but not tonight. Tonight was for coon hunting. Sharon was settled down now and finally noticed Art's new binoculars and asked if she could look at them. Without thinking, he handed them to her; she pulled off her upturned glasses and planted them squarely on her eyes. Two of the most perfectly matched rings were left right where she had placed them. Handing back the binoculars and replacing her glasses, she leaned over to kiss Grandpa on top of his head and asked how she looked. She was back in a tizzy, as she could hear Billy Bob's car come to a stop and the southern rabble horn sounded out. Grandpa looked up at her, gasping, she thought, at how good she looked, but Grandpa said she looked just perfect. Out the door she flew, barely taking time to grab a jacket.

Grandpa's next words were to tell the boys they had better skedaddle. You could hear the front screen door slam shut as the side door slammed open, with Sharon busting in, screaming and crying at the same time, "I am going to kill them two heathens! I am going to kill them." You see, the boys had been playing tricks on her for a long time now. Things like putting frogs in her bathtub after Grandpa had just installed indoor plumbing. Putting garter snakes in her purse to be found later when she and her girlfriends went shopping. Grandma, seeing what had happened, rushed to her aid and started wiping the coal dust off and smiling a little at the same time. Grandma was more interested in what was on Sharon's ring finger. Sure enough, Billy Bob had proposed and given her a ring without even noticing just what she looked like—the biggest raccoon in Meigs County.

Billy Bob followed Sharon into the house, all sheepish and shy-like, with his hands in his pockets, waiting for the approval of Grandpa and Grandma. They welcomed him to the family with open arms; they had known him for most of his life. Everything was settled down, Sharon was floating on air, and all of her dreams had come true. She could never stay mad at the boys for anything, as she truly loved them.

The boys were somewhat concerned about what might happen when this night was over and discussed the possibilities. Art did inform Dick that it was an accident. He had forgotten about putting coal dust on the binoculars, or so he said. Traveling along the dirt road to the cornfield gate, they could see and hear Billy Bob's car leave Grandpa's. It was then they realized they had left without Frosty, the best coon dog in Meigs County. Grandpa had won the county coon-hunting contest with him for the last two years in a row. Well, anyway, it was back to untie Frosty and set him on his way. Frosty took off down the lane, across the oil-soaked county road, under the gate of Grandpa's neighbor's cornfield, and up his long hollow. He was already starting to howl, being hot on the trail. The boys did not waste any time crossing the road and over the gate and up the long, dark hollow. They had never hunted this hollow before. It wasn't too much longer before they began wondering just where they were. They had lost the sound of Frosty. They decided the best thing to do was just sit down and wait until Frosty alerted them of a treed raccoon.

It was a beautiful night. The fall weather was just perfect, and they stretched out on the ground, looking up at the stars. Of course, their thoughts went to what they had just seen on TV. "It was supposed to be good luck if you saw a shooting star," said Dick.

"I don't know," said Art. "That might be a spaceship moving out there."

"Do you think aliens might come here?" asked Dick.

"I don't know. Why would an alien come here? Besides, Grandpa would just get his gun and shoot them if they did come here," replied Art. "What's that?"

Art could hear the faint howl of Frosty way up the hollow and off to the right. Luckily, the dirt road continued along the edge of the cornfield from where the farmer had used it to tend his fields. On up the hollow they went. By this time, clouds had rolled in and blocked all the stars and moonlight. It did not matter; they had their flashlights anyway. In a great hurry now, they rushed to greet Frosty with his treed coon. Nearing the top of the ridge, where Frosty had the coon treed, a great spotlight was beaming down from the heavens, traversing back and forth as if looking for something. The boys felt sure the beam would eventually find them and beam them up. After hearing what Walter Cronkite had to say, the boys were in a total panic.

Grabbing Frosty by the collar, off the hill the boys ran. They ran as hard and as fast as they could go, down the dirt road, through, not under the gate, across the oily road, and down the gravel road to Grandpa's house.

This time, the screen door really slammed hard, along with the main door. They were out of breath and could not talk. At first, Grandpa was really worried about what could be wrong. He had to get them to settle down. He was worried that they may have accidentally shot somebody or maybe someone's cow. Could they have gotten Frosty hurt? Grandpa was not a drinking man nowadays, but he knew when somebody needed a strong drink. He got out his bottle of Jack Daniel's and made them take just a sip. "It's not as good as my homemade stuff that I used to make, but it will do." Grandpa used to be the number-one moonshiner in southern Ohio with his hidden room, but that will be covered later on. Right now, he needed to get the boys to settle down.

With one more sip each, the boys got a hold of themselves. "Aliens are after us," said Art. "Yes," said Dick, "they are. Don't laugh, they really are."

The Foot Brothers

Grandpa realized he had a serious problem on his hands. "I told you boys there are no such things here on Earth. Now tell me what happened for you to think the aliens are after you." "Well," said Art, "we followed Frosty across the road onto Old Man Hoy's farm. He was hot on the tracks of a coon; I know he was. He must have lost the trail somewhere up past the cornfield, 'cause he finally treed him on top of the third ridge up the hollow. Dick and I were not too far behind, but when we got there, a huge spotlight was shining down from heaven, trying to locate Frosty and us."

"Maybe they were going to beam us up and do all kinds of stuff to us. You don't know, Grandpa," said Dick. "Oh, yes I do know," said Grandpa. "You boys go get in the truck, and I will get my coat. We will get to the bottom of this great mystery."

The boys would not leave the house, even though they still had the gun and a bullet. But with Grandpa leading the way, out the door they went. "Aren't you going to get your gun?" asked Art. "Nope, don't need one," said Grandpa.

Dick was planning his move so he could be seated in the middle of Grandpa's 1951 Chevy truck. If aliens did get them, they would have to go through Grandpa or Art before they got him. Besides, he would not have to get out and open the gate at Old Man Hoy's place. One less chance for the aliens to get him.

With the gears grinding, they headed down the lane, across the oily road, onto the dirt road, and up to the gate. Grandpa told Art to get out and open the gate. After some scuffling with Dick, he finally made a break for the gate. He jumped out and threw it open and got right back in the truck. Grandpa said, "Old Man Hoy does not have cows anymore, so just leave it open. We will close it when we come back."

Boy, was Art relieved! On up the dirt road they went, across the creek, with Grandpa following an old logging road to the top of the hill. It was still there, the spaceship, still looking for Art and Dick with its spotlight. "Look, Grandpa, we told you! Be careful. Do you want to take our gun?"

Parking the truck, Grandpa got out, looked around, and told the boys to get out. Wondering why Grandpa was not scared out of his skin, the boys got out—of course, sliding across the truck seat to go out the same door Grandpa did and to be as close as they could to him. Grandpa informed them of what they were really looking at. "Boys," he said, "what you are seeing is the reflection of the lights from Big Muskie, a strip mine dragline used to uncover coal. The lights are reflecting off the clouds, back down to Earth. See, as it turns to drop a load of dirt and goes back for another load, they are destroying the very ground we live on. The lights are so far away and so high up in the air that by the time it gets here, with the angles that it makes, the light travels very fast. Now you know what it is."

The boys knew of the Big Muskie, as they had taken a field trip from school to look at it. What could they say now? They felt stupid, they were embarrassed, but most of all they felt relieved that aliens

The Foot Brothers

were not about to arrive here on Earth. They all piled into the truck for the trip home, laughing and joking with each other about what just happened.

"Another thing," said Grandpa. "Up in Alaska, where there is a lot of ice and snow and clouds, airport runway lights have been known to do this. Their lights have reflected off ice clouds, that's clouds full of ice crystals; anyway, these clouds reflect the light forty or fifty miles away. This has caused planes to crash. The pilot thought the lights on the ground was the runway, but it was not. Even down south in Texas, in the wintertime, an ice cloud can form, and car lights reflecting off a pond can cause the same effect."

"Wait a minute," said Art. "I hear Frosty, and he has a raccoon treed." Sure enough, down at the bottom of the hill, there was Frosty, sitting at the bottom of a large oak tree and howling away. In the excitement, everybody had forgotten about him.

Grandpa told Dick to get out and take care of it. Art gave him the gun; he already had the bullet. This was the first time he got to shoot the gun. "What a big pelt he will make. I bet he will bring twenty-five dollars," said Grandpa.

Everybody was very happy; they would have plenty of money for Christmas. Hurrying home to let Grandma know what was going on, all three started dreaming up stories to tell her. "We had better not," stated Grandpa. "You boys just went through letting your imagination get carried away. I don't need her doing that."

Back at the house, they explained to Grandma what had happened. She seemed a little disappointed in the whole story. Grandpa was back in his rocker, Dick was back in Grandpa's lap, and Art was back on the coal bucket. Grandpa was going to give them one more word of wisdom. "You know, boys, this Earth is God's nursery. He put us here so we could grow, have more children, and someday we could go be with Him. He would never permit another soul-bearing creature into His nursery, would He?" This little bit of wisdom would stay with the boys the rest of their lives. With this wisdom, Dick fell asleep in Grandpa's lap, to be woken up in the summer of 1964 (As nothing exciting happened for the next seven years.)

Chapter 2

Art was graduating in the spring of sixty-four, and both boys knew this was going to be the end of their carefree days. Art had inquired at the local air force recruitment station as to what they had to offer, as he wanted to get out and see the world. He had checked with the other services, but none offered the training he wanted. Being somewhat of a ladies' man, he had a girlfriend in every county and town up and down the river. At least he thought he was a ladies' man, anyway. He wanted a job that would impress the ladies even more. With the world at peace in the spring of 1964, there could be no better time for him to complete his military obligation. Art decided that he and Dick could goof off all summer and he could join up in the fall. Art did have a car and a driver's license, so they could go anyplace they wanted. All they had to do was steal gas from the old farmers' tractors. Looking back on this, it seemed so stupid, with gas costing only thirteen cents a gallon during gas wars. Maybe they could find Grandpa's old moonshine still, maybe run off a batch or two, play more tricks on Sharon, who knows, just generally raise hell all summer. Little did he realize that by the spring of sixty-five, all hell would break loose in a little country called Vietnam.

Arthur Jude with Dick Hoy

One Saturday in early September, Grandpa thought everyone had gone to the county fair. Grandma was always entering her pickled eggs. He decided he should clean up his old still. Everybody thought the only reason he married Grandma was because she made such good pickled eggs. She never did win any prizes, though. Little did Grandpa know that Art had stayed behind and was in the hayloft with one of his hussies. A hidden door in the back of the barn wall opened to a little room with a set of stairs going down into what looked like a little dungeon, from what Art could see peeking over the bales of hay. The boys had been looking for this hideout for years; it was perfect. A person could not tell that the back wall had a hidden room with a basement. The barn was built with the back half on top of a little hill, with the front supported by posts so the livestock could find some shelter.

From what Art could figure out, this must be the old root cellar of years ago. Grandpa must have blocked up the entrance from the overhang years ago. The pigpen was directly behind the barn. With the smells coming from that place, the bales of hay stacked, most of the time, in front of the back wall, one could never find it. Grandpa worked away, cleaning and shining, up and down the steps, cussing the cobwebs from years of neglect. Every now and then, Grandpa would stop and go out the front door, as if waiting and looking for someone.

Sure enough, his younger brother Cliff from over Point Pleasant and their brother Doug from up in Pomeroy way came slowly up the drive. Cliff was a coal-truck driver, and Doug was the Meigs County sheriff. Art figured out the whole scheme. Grandpa would make the shine. His brother Cliff would distribute it over in West Virginia, and their brother Doug could warn them of any danger. No wonder they never got caught! All the catfishing these three had done on the Ohio River, or the so-called catfishing, was just a cover for their moonshining operation. Cliff was telling Grandpa about a problem he had with some kids parking in his cornfield. They were driving over his corn and pretty much destroying

The Foot Brothers

the crop. He really did not care about some high school kids going back in there and parking. He just didn't want his corn torn up; it was almost ready to harvest. Cliff asked Grandpa if he knew of any way of keeping those kids out of there without too much work involved. "Do you remember what we did to those Hathaway kids years ago? They did not come back here for years."

"What was that?" asked Doug. Cliff just broke out laughing, "Come on, tell me!" asked Doug emphatically. "Well," said Grandpa, "years ago, the Hathaway family came over one evening for a visit around Halloween time, I reckon. Cliff and I took a sheet of white canvas out of the old man's storage shed, hid out down behind the pine tree that used be along the lane. When they were leaving, we put the sheet over us, jumped out to the edge of the road, then ducked back behind the pine tree and off into the darkness. I didn't think it would work that good, but it must have scared the hell out of them. When they got home, they called the sheriff and then called us about something being in our front yard. Man, was it a big to-do! The sheriff looked for hours for whatever was in our front yard." "Oh, yes, that is the same woman that I sent her husband a doctor's report I had stolen out of a trash bin of her being some nut case. I don't mention that too often."

Every question of Art's life had been answered now as to why he was the way he was. He was Grandpa all over again. He was looking forward to the rest of his life. What excitement must be in store for him! The old men were slowly putting things back where they were and mumbling about how much shine they should run this fall; it had been a while. They finally left the barn on their way to the river for a night of fishing. Art spent the rest of the evening in the hayloft with his floozy.

The next day, Art told Dick all about what the old men said and what he had seen.

Art was ready to make his mark on this world; he convinced Dick they should take care of Grandpa Cliff's problem. He knew exactly where

Cliff was referring to, as he had used the place before. He also thought he might know the girl, but he was not sure. After casing the place and asking a few questions of his friends, they both figured that Friday night was going to be the next opportunity for them. But what to do? Both boys were new to this. How could they scare these two kids so bad that they never came back? "I know," said Art. "We will get a sheet from Grandma's closet and use it like Grandpa did with the canvas. Yes, this is it. We will get a sheet, go over to Grandpa Cliff's farm early in the afternoon, and about the edge of dark, we will sneak into the cornfield. We will wait for them to drive back there. After they jump into the back seat, I will put the sheet over me and jump up on the trunk of the car. I will jump up and down, hollering and screaming like a monkey. That ought to do it."

It seemed like they would never arrive; it must have been eleven o'clock. The boys were still used to going to bed early. The excitement they felt was unbelievable. Grandpa would be proud. Even Grandpa Cliff would think very highly of them.

The car came to a rolling stop after tearing down some corn stalks. It did not take long for the occupants to jump over the front seat with clothes flying in every direction. "Man," whispered Art, "I did not know that girl had such big boobs." "Get your mind back on what we are doing," whispered Dick. With that comment, Art veiled himself in the sheet and jumped on top of the car's trunk with sounds and movements like a demon from hell.

The boys had often wondered how and what those two felt, being in the predicament they were in. They guessed it was one of those things you just don't talk about, just like the doctor's form Grandpa stole and filled out that almost caused a divorce. With all the commotion inside the car and the actions of Art on top of the car, the two occupants finally were back in the front seat, still without their clothes. He managed to get the car started, and down the path they went with Art still on top, but not for long. Art came rolling off, a few feet farther on. Grandma's sheet was not

The Foot Brothers

so lucky; it went on down the road, caught on the rear antenna. "Those two had to think something was chasing them, don't you think?" asked Art. (This really happened when Art was home on leave in 1966 or 1967.)

Chapter 3

Mothman statue in Point Pleasant, W.V.

The Foot Brothers

Years later, a movie was made of this incident, *The Moth Man with the Silver Bridge*. Sometimes, it's best just to keep one's mouth shut. Grandma's sheet was never seen again. She wondered for years where that sheet went.

A couple of days later, Art joined the air force. As you recall, he wanted to get out and see the world. He ended up in North Dakota, working underground on nuclear-tipped ICBMs. Two years later, Dick finished high school. We all know what was going on in 1966. He came home in 1968, all in one piece. The local fiberglass factory was hiring, so Dick figured it was as good as any place to work. Art, on the other hand, figured he was as safe as anyone could be during these times, so he stayed in the air force for the next twenty-some years.

In the fall of 1987, Art came home. Grandma and Grandpa were both gone, and even Billy Bob had suffered an early demise. Sharon had moved into or more or less stayed at Grandma and Grandpa's place. She felt safe there. Dick was married with three kids of his own, but he always found time to take extra care of Sharon. He would do her banking for her and fix things around the place. She would fix for him and deliver his lunch on the days he worked. Art, on the other hand, had been through five divorces. Even though he had a retirement income from the military, all of it was spent on alimony even before he got it. Needless to say, he was down and out. He asked Sharon if he could move in with her for a little while.

Dick could not believe the gravity of Art's plight. He offered to get him a job at the fiberglass plant where he worked. As it worked out, it felt like this was supposed to have been in the first place. The boys were content now; they even went coon hunting late that fall, and they reminisced about what they used to do. Art finally admitted to Dick that he was the one who had nailed the panties and bra of a girl Dick had the hots for to the tree on the on the big curve going into town.

Things were going well for both boys, but they could not stand just going to work, as that was very boring. Dick had a good job at the factory because he had been there so many years. Art's job, on the other hand, was an entry-level job for a younger man. They were searching for something to get into when their cousin Mike showed up one winter day. Everybody liked Mike; he was the smartest of all the relatives. You never dared to get into a conversation with him trying to outwit him; it just could not be done. The man could have been a brain surgeon if he had left southern Ohio.

Mike was a great hunter; he had been out west hunting elk and to Alaska hunting grizzly bears. Mike was honest to a fault, too honest and forthright. He mentioned one day that he believed there could be a Bigfoot roaming the hills of southern Ohio, just like the ones they had out in Washington and Oregon. The boys were just stunned. All these years trying to keep up with Mike; they finally found the opportunity they had been looking for.

People at work wondered what Art and Dick were up to. It was time for the spring turkey hunt of 1988. They all figured by the way Art was strutting about that it was some kind of strange way of attracting turkeys; little did they know. Even Sharon had some kind of inkling that the boys were up to something. She was not about to be left out in the cold this time, after all the years of suffering the brunt of their pranks. She demanded to be a part of whatever was going on. The boys finally broke down and told her.

They were going to pull a Bigfoot joke on Mike. Sharon was ecstatic; she could not wait. Mike had been another thorn in her side, not that he pulled pranks on her or treated her badly. He was so much smarter and more quick-witted than anyone else. She thought if all three of them stuck together, they just might pull this off.

The planning was started; Art was to rent the gorilla outfit. He would be the one wearing the outfit and running across the top of the hill. Sharon was to plan a birthday party for all the little kids down at Mike's house. She wanted to make sure she had her movie camera. She was always doing this anyway. And besides, a perfect hill was right across the road from Mike's house. Bigfoot could run across the top of the hill. Timing was everything. The birthday party would start inside at exactly two thirty; Sharon was to get everybody outside, so she could film them better in the sunlight. Dick was in charge of making the foot or feet that they would use in making the footprints that "Bigfoot" would leave behind. Dick's feet were perfect; he had cut them out of a sheet of plywood. He laid his arm and hand down on the plywood and marked around it. When he first cut them out, he was concerned about a left and right; to his surprise, all he had to do was turn one of them over. When he ended up, they were about fourteen inches long and eight inches wide, just perfect. Being very discreet, they all would meet at night and develop the walking and running actions of Art wearing the outfit. Art got the actions down perfectly. They even sat down and wrote out a time frame when everything was supposed to happen.

Early Saturday morning, when Mike was still at work, all three drove down to the next dirt road, where "Bigfoot" would have had to cross from running off the top of the hill. This was a perfect place to plant the feet. There was a little creek, the dirt road, and a twelve-foot soft dirt embankment up the other side, going off into the woods.

Of course, all plans of mice and men go astray. The first thing to do was make some good footprints into the dirt along the edge of the road. Crack went the first foot; it broke right in two. The dirt was too hard or Dick hit the foot with the rock too hard. It did not matter; they still had one good foot. Knowing now what they had to do, they found softer dirt to implant the footprint. Art pointed out that "Bigfoot" would have to weigh nine hundred pounds for him to make an impression like that.

Big Foot footprint in mud; Big Foot plywood mold

Sharon was really getting into this by now. On the embankment where "Bigfoot" went up, she got her hatchet out and made claws on the end of Bigfoot's toes. They did a good job. The footprints were spaced about six feet apart. Erasing any sign that someone had been there, they went back to Sharon's house. They also parked their car inside the barn where nobody could see it.

It was getting to be about twelve o'clock. Art and Dick did not want Mike to see them at Sharon's house, so they took off on the four-wheeler to the back of the hill. There they waited for two thirty and Sharon to come out into the front yard and start filming. Art had the outfit on. He was hoping and praying no one would shoot him. In the meantime, Sharon saw Mike and reminded him of the birthday party, saying he has to be there. Everything was going as planned. At two thirty, Sharon and all

The Foot Brothers

the kids went out of the house. With Sharon's coaxing, Mike finally went out of the house too. He was a little bit of a ham anyway; he liked to be in any movie footage. He was also the best looking of all the family. Now you know all the reasons why they wanted to trick him.

Art in Big Foot costume

Arthur Jude with Dick Hoy

Art came out from behind a large tree in full costume, arms swinging, and taking steps as large as he could take. He must have gone fifty yards across the top of that hill, then over the ridge toward the location where the footprints were located. Of course, he couldn't wait to get out of that gorilla outfit; he was covered in sweat. Hidden by the ridge, Art and Dick waited until they heard the car take off with Sharon and Mike in hot pursuit in the direction that Bigfoot was headed. They took a peek over the ridge to make sure the coast was clear. They could barely see Sharon's car turning up the dirt road. The boys got on that four-wheeler and got out of there as fast as they could. They then drove over to the next county to wait it out and to make sure nobody saw them.

Sharon and Mike, with one or two other adults who had seen Bigfoot, arrived at the scene of the crime, if you will. Mike took charge, of course, instructing all not to destroy any evidence or disturb any markings that were left behind. Sharon reassured Mike that she had him on tape. They tried to measure his gait, impressed by his weight as the footprints implied; the length of his claws, from the impressions on the embankment. To give this a final air, which the boys had nothing to do with, someone's coonhound on top of the next ridge cut loose as if he was on his last coon hunt. That sealed it for Mike; he had seen a Bigfoot. The other two people agreed with Mike; they too had seen Bigfoot. To give this more credibility, Sharon kept the movie camera running all the time, hoping to capture conversations.

It was all planned. Art and Dick were to come to Sharon's house at five o'clock, and this would give everybody time to settle down. By this time, Mike would have figured everything out. He could take a joke as well as anybody.

The one problem? In all the planning they did, they did not plan an end to all this stuff. Another problem: the kids had seen "Bigfoot." The other adults also saw.

The Foot Brothers

They all showed up at Sharon's house, Art and Dick too. Mike was positive he had seen Bigfoot. "What should we do, call the newspaper? Call the television station? We have to tell the world what we seen. We have it on tape. They can't call us a buncha idiots!" Art and Dick were at a loss as to what to do. Sharon got out the ice cream and cake left over from the birthday party. Art finally could not stand it anymore. He went out to his truck and put the gorilla suit on, and back in the house he went. He thought Mike would knock him out. Mike took it in good humor. The only thing Mike ever said was, "You should not do a person like that." Art felt bad, and so did everybody else; one would think that would be the end of this escapade, but not so.

A week later, *The Columbus Dispatch* ran an article about "Bigfoot" on the front page of the local section. (To read the articles in *The Columbus Dispatch*, look at the dates 5/8/88 1C and 5/25/88 1C). There were over four hundred people in Meigs County looking for you-know-who. They had shotguns and trained tracking dogs; participants claimed they would not leave until they either captured or shot Bigfoot.

The local Ford dealer was having a contest on homemade videos for his advertisement campaign. No one knows who did it, but "Bigfoot" was seen on television, running across the top of the hill. Surely this had to end, Art and Dick agreed. The best thing for them to do now was keep their mouths shut. Little did they know, mothers with teenage daughters would meet them at the school-bus stop, so Bigfoot would not get them. College students at Ohio University in Athens formed block-watch groups and developed the buddy system when they went out at night. This was the start of the Bigfoot legend in Meigs County. Even the major T.V. channel listed Meigs County as a sighting location of Bigfoot. Art and Dick wisely decided not to discuss this anymore.

Art was getting his life back together; he had a steady job now, thanks to Dick. He had run into an old girlfriend, Shirley, and they decided to get married. She had never been married, and with Art's history of martial

Arthur Jude with Dick Hoy

success, it was doubtful she could change him. Things were going OK for the boys, but life was boring, with all the uproar over. Art did settle down, bought a small house, and started raising prize hogs at Sharon's farm while still working every day. Dick was busy raising his family; they would stop for beers every now and then after work.

Chapter 4

By 1999, the boys had had about enough. There was no excitement in their lives. One winter day, Art, out at the smoke booth at work, casually mentioned that he was "Bigfoot." Paul, a low-level supervisor, quickly informed Art, "People go to hell for lying." For some reason, it just seemed like everyone at work was envious of Art and Dick's relationship. They would sneak around corners, trying to listen to what Art and Dick were talking about. There were other brothers who worked there, but they did not even talk to each other. Dick had worked there for almost thirty years, Art was a newbie; maybe that's what it was.

One day in early spring, Art mentioned to Dick that his new wife, Shirley, believed in aliens. She thought they were actually here on Earth now. "That isn't nothing," replied Dick. "My wife and half my family believe aliens have been coming to Earth for years. They even think aliens have interbred with humans."

"Have they ever seen a UFO?" asked Art.

"I don't know. I will ask."

At the same time, the boys came to the same conclusion, remembering back to their days of supposedly seeing a UFO. Which one were they going to trick first, Shirley or Billy? It had to be Billy, they decided; it was going to be easier setting the whole thing up. Dick had property on the lake, and his youngest son, who was also a believer, was going off to the military by the first of July. The lake property was perfect; it had a clubhouse just right for the party, controlled entry, and was way out in the country, just down the road from Salt Fork State Park. Nobody took notice of what anybody was doing. There were plenty of side roads for a person to get lost on. Dick had been planning a party for a long time now. He had asked Sharon to come down and do the filming of the party, but being at night and all the beer drinking, she thought it best not to. The only time the boys would talk about this was at work or in the bar over beers. The best place for them to talk was at the bar that opened up at six in the morning, the Cedar Street Grill. Art and Dick had to work a month of nights and then a month of days, with twelve-hour shifts. That was hard work. They did not want anybody to know what they were doing. Every now and then, the boys would ask people at work what they thought about aliens. They would get some of the strangest stories you ever heard.

Sharon was surprised to see the boys that early on a cold March morning, but she was always glad to see them. She had been living on the old farmstead for a long time. Art keep his prize hogs there; he had them on an automatic feeder, Sharon just had to look after them. The boys asked Sharon if they could use the old barn to build an invention they had thought up. It was a perpetual-motion machine, they told her. Sharon was not the sharpest tack in the box, but she knew the boys were up to something. She always seemed agitated at the boys for all the tricks they played on her, but that did make her the center of attention, which she dearly loved. She was active in her church and was the one who made sure all birthdays were celebrated and filmed.

The Foot Brothers

Cleaning up the secret room in the barn took some time, what with moving the old still out of the way and removing the hangers where Grandpa hung up all the deer he had poached. Sharon thought they were going to fire up the still or get back into poaching again. She dared not ask; she was only hoping to be a part of what was going to happen. Sharon had never had kids of her own, so she thought of Art and Dick as hers. On her mantel, she even kept pictures of the boys when they were little.

Art's job was to build the spaceship. Being in the air force gave him an insight into what he thought a spaceship should look like. Dick's job was to come up with what they thought an alien footprint would look like. The first thing Art would need was some helium, we all know what is filled with helium, and if it's light enough it will float through the air. His second requirement was a large balloon. At the party store, Art purchased a four-foot balloon. It was gray in color, but Art had planned on painting it anyway. It had to have porthole windows and lights on the bottom, to make it look like an engine was located there. Yes, it had a light-ray engine; that way it could travel at the speed of light. Art was pretty proud of his accomplishments so far. While blowing the balloon up, things were looking really good, until *boom*, the damn thing blew up and scared the crap out of Art. He had gotten the balloon up to about five feet. Art wondered if the people at Cape Canaveral experienced the same feelings.

Oh well, off to the Internet to find companies that make larger balloons. South Carolina was the home of several companies that sold large balloons, if you wanted to make one yourself. A ten-footer was on sale, just what Art wanted. As quickly as it arrived, Art was back at the barn with it. He had lost most of the helium during the explosion, so he had to go get more. Art started filling this spaceship up more slowly and cautiously. It was a perfect size; it would fit nicely in the back of a U-Haul truck, about eleven feet in diameter. The only problem was, how could he hold it in place while they painted it? Fish netting would do the trick.

Back to the Internet. In the state of Washington were all kinds of netting suppliers. It worked perfectly, with a little trimming. There it was, an almost-perfect spaceship. Now for the painting. This ship could accommodate at least eleven portholes as windows and had plenty of room at the bottom for the light-ray engine. The balloon was already red, so all the boys had to paint were the white portholes; of course, they used reflective paint. They painted a black edge around the portholes and where the aircraft door was located. Dick also painted some insignias on the lower sides. Art hooked up LEDs, the type that flashed on and off, red ones and some green ones and a blue one at each porthole, using nine-volt batteries. The lights for the engine were installed, but they stayed on all the time. With a little bit of duct tape to hold down the wires and to keep the net in place, it was perfect, Art also taped a note to the bottom of the ship: WHAT THIS NOTE SAYS IS TOP SECRET. He did hope someday someone finds it.

Of course, the boys were drinking beer all time they were working on the spaceship, so it was their opinion just how good it looked. They had repaired the door on the barn and installed a large lock so nobody could get in.

About the first of April, the spaceship was complete. The boys had made several trips to the lake, testing small, store-bought balloons to make sure they would fly from the lake in the direction of the clubhouse. There was always a breeze blowing off the lake, up the hollow toward the clubhouse. With the clubhouse about fifteen hundred feet from the lake, they wanted to make sure the spaceship would not go out of sight before it reached the clubhouse. They found a perfect spot to set the spaceship off; large pine trees lined both sides of the road, closer to the lake but in line with the clubhouse, it was just right.

The Foot Brothers

Note taped to spaceship: REWARD FOR RETURN

What would you call them?, molds, foot print impression models, anyway its use is to form whatever is left behind as your footprint. Dick came up with the perfect footprint material: rebar, the steel used in reinforcing concrete. With the little flanges on the side, the ability to stretch it out and flatten it, he could make all different sizes and shapes. No two would ever be the same. Different diameters are available if you want to make older-looking or younger-looking footprints. The heel was just a circle welded together, about the size of an ordinary human's heel. The toes, however, resembled a chicken's toes, much longer than human toes and only three. Using three different sizes of rebar for toes did give the footprint a lifelike appearance. Art could not help but reminded Dick that was his secret name, Chicken Foot. No wonder he did such a good job. Dick did flatten out the end of one of the toes to help out whoever found the footprints. That was to get them thinking maybe this could be an alien footprint. Everybody has seen *E.T.* Dick made several pairs and welded a long rod handle on top so he could implant the footprints anywhere he wanted.

Alien footprints in mud; Alien foot mold

Dick could not wait to test his footprint. On April 20, 1999, he headed for the golf course located next to the lake. The alien footprint makers were hidden well inside his golf bag. Finding a suitable place on the back

The Foot Brothers

nine, Dick headed over the hill to the edge of the lake. This location was not perfect, as it was the tail end of a hollow about the lake, and all kinds of critters found their way in there. This was just a test anyway. Dick got the knack of placing footprints in all kinds of mud—just how hard to press down, which set to use, how far to start having the footprints out in the water so they could walk to shore. He must have made a hundred footprints on that muddy bank.

He was unconcerned about the footprints left behind; a rain would wash them away, and besides, nobody ever went in that hollow anyway. You know all plans of mice and men go astray. But, as plans go wrong, the footprints were found by two old fishermen. This lake resort had more than its share of retired folks living there. Most of these people had nothing better to do than dream of the things that could have been or things they could have accomplished in their younger days. Please keep in mind the boys did not think anybody would find the footprints, so they did not know anything about what was going on with the footprints. Being found by the two old men was probably the worst thing that could happen—or the best thing, depending on how you want to look at it. Curiosity got the best of the old men; they wondered what could have made such impressions in the mud.

Mustering all their thought and knowledge, they decided to contact the park ranger to come and look at the footprints. He did not know what they were, but he had a friend from Montana visiting the park who was a trained archaeologist. Maybe he would know. All four of them went back the next day to investigate "the site," as it was now being called. The archaeologist was at a loss as to what they were. He reassured them the prints were from some type of large bird. However, the only ones he knew of that looked like these were some prehistoric bird that lived in South America thousands of years ago. From the size of the footprints and the depth they were implanted in the mud, the largest must be about four feet tall and weigh about forty-five pounds, the smallest about three feet tall and weighing about thirty pounds.

"Who knows?" said the archaeologist. "Maybe that bird did not go extinct. Maybe it's been living here in this lake for all these years. Maybe it's like the lungfish in Africa. It can bury itself in mud and live for years there." More than curiosity flowed from the archaeologist now. He went and got his camera and some plaster of Paris. Using a complete package of instamatic film on the footprints and making enough plaster of Paris imprints of them, he was satisfied he could get to the bottom of this. He did give the fishermen one of the photos, though not a very good one, of the footprints, but he claimed there were not enough plaster of Paris imprints to go around. By now, the old men were out of their skins. They could capture this thing and become famous, maybe even rich! That became their summer quest: search the lake every day in hopes of capturing this amazing creature.

Chapter 5

The big day had arrived, June 6. The party was set, Dick had made ready the camera, and made sure Billy would be on the patio at ten thirty. She was to be the bartender, even though she did not drink. This was the time they figured the spaceship would fly over the clubhouse. He also made sure all of his kids were there, especially his son who was going off to war; the party was for him. He, like his mother, was a believer.

Art was having a frantic day. He had to be at the lake and set the spaceship off at exactly ten twenty-five. Having parked the U-Haul in the barn where no one would see him loading the spaceship, he realized he needed help. The only person available was his cousin Mike, who was glad to be a part of a new hoax. Maybe people would remember he was the one not being tricked this time and was in on the tricking. He also brought along his brother Doug, Grandpa's brother's offspring. They did not know anything about the secret room. By the time they removed enough of the wall for the spaceship to fit through, it was time to leave.

Dick, on the other hand, was having a good day. He did find time to sneak out to an island in the lake, the one right in line with the pine trees and the clubhouse and the hollow. He was very careful on how he planted the footprints this time. Staying on the boat as long as he could, he started placing the footprints on the lake bottom, to make it look like they walked out of the lake onto the beach. Motoring down to a spot where he could get out on the ground without leaving footprints, he went back to his original spot and finished making footprints that led onto grass and into the woods up to a very old beech tree. This tree had been hit by lightning years ago, and the top had been burned out. He made damn sure no telltale signs were left of him being there.

Art, driving the truck, timed everything down to a T. They had gotten to the lake with a few minutes to spare. The only thing out of place was that Art had seen lights out on the lake. From the shadows, they appeared to be fishermen in small boats. One of them had a spotlight shining on the shore, as if they were looking for something. *Oh well, just a bunch of old men catfishing.* It was still a long way around the lake. As a matter of fact, they passed by the spot where the launch pad was, the spot with the large pine trees that hung over the road. Finding a good location to turn around and to recheck his timing, they had a few minutes to wait. Doug, the brave one, volunteered to sit in back of the U-Haul, holding the spaceship, ready to launch it out of the back as soon as they were stopped and the door was opened. While they were waiting for the correct timing, everything was double-checked; all lights were on, the pressure in the spaceship was checked, and everything was ready.

Art timed the cars that went by. *Too many cars*, thought Art. "We have to do this quickly." Down the road they went, and sure enough, as quickly as they stopped, a van with a family in it stopped and asked if they needed help. Art replied, "No," in a rougher tone than he normally used. On down the road the car went, leaving the road as dark as could be. Art looked out for any signs of the boats or lights; nothing. Mike and Art jumped out of the truck, rushed around to the back, threw up the door, and out came Doug with the spaceship. Up the ship went, almost getting caught in the tops of the pine trees. Taking only a few seconds,

The Foot Brothers

they were out of there. All three were breaking their necks looking out the windows, trying to see exactly where the ship had gone as they raced down the road.

That old U-Haul did not go very fast, but no more than ten minutes in their trip back home, two carloads of rangers were headed back toward the lake. Art was sure they were caught; the rangers would turn around and get them any minute. He pulled off the road at an old gas station, where they could buy a Coke and wait. Twenty minutes went by, and nobody showed up. On down the road they went. Back out on the freeway to home, Art looked in his rearview mirror and saw three highway patrol cars coming at high speed, with lights flashing. For sure this time he thought they were caught, but they did not get pulled over. The highway patrol just flew by them. Getting back to the barn was a relief; all three wondered where the spaceship went. Fixing the wall before they left really helped.

Art could not wait until the next time for work so Dick could fill him in on what happened. The first thing out of Dick's mouth was, "Where were you? Did you do it?" Disappointed, Art could not believe all that work went for nothing. He filled Dick in about the park rangers, and Dick realized Art had been there. Dick informed Art that a couple of drunks had gotten into the park and knocked over some trashcans, and someone had called the law. They both wondered what had happened to the spaceship and for the next three weeks they wondered what had happened to the spaceship. Dick spent every minute he could at the lake. Art even came down so they could hang out in bars, hoping to hear anything about what happened, but there was nothing except the usual. All sorts of people start visiting the lake this time of year. Even the group that only wore white shirts and black pants did not seem out of place. The women who were with them dressed the same. With all the Mennonite people moving in around there, even they did not look out of place.

Arthur Jude with Dick Hoy

Little did they know, the two old fishermen, in their quest to find and capture the prehistoric bird, had been out on the lake the night of June 6, 1999. As a matter of fact, they were the ones with the spotlight. Did they see anything? You bet they did. They saw almost the entire episode, from far away though. From where they were located, across the lake, it looked like the spaceship had taken off from the island. That night of June 6, not even a breeze was stirring. After the spaceship cleared the pine trees, it must have lost some altitude from being cooled down under the trees. Once it got out in the open over the lake, it started warming back up. Slowly it rose as it traveled over to the center of the lake and off into the heavens. (Please be warned that doing this is illegal. This balloon or spaceship can go as high as sixty thousand feet, staying aloft for up to fourteen days. It could interfere with aircraft.) To this day, the boys wonder where the spaceship landed.

Cautiously, with gun in hand, the old men approached the island. Circling and spotlighting at the same time, they finally noticed the footprints leaving the water. What to do now? They were totally confused. Is it a prehistoric bird or is it something from outer space? They did not have the guts to investigate at night like this; nor did they want their chance for fame and fortune to slip away. They decided to stay on the boat all night, taking turns sleeping. Their families must have worried about them.

Somehow, they made it through the night. At the crack of dawn, both were wide awake and full of excitement. Would they be the ones to capture this thing, whatever it was? Circling the island one more time, they could not see anything out of the ordinary, just the footprints. Gaining all the courage they could from their bottle of Jack Daniel's, they waded ashore. Searching and looking, looking and searching, they did not find anything except the footprints. What to do now? What made the footprints? What kind of flying machine did they see last night? Both of the old men liked to think they have their feet planted squarely on the

The Foot Brothers

ground. They decided to go home, get a good day's rest, not tell anyone what they saw, come back later that evening, and reinvestigate everything before they came to any conclusions. Telling someone what they saw at their age could land them in a nursing home.

Who could they trust? There was only one thing this could be: *aliens*. Nothing could last for thousands of years in the bottom of this lake, could it? What they had seen flying over the lake, with lights flashing, could be only one thing, a spaceship. They were convinced, but what to do, who to tell?

They contacted the man from Montana directly, and he arrived the next day with a camera and more plaster of Paris. This time he was distant and aloof, taking photos and making impressions, treating the old fishermen as second-class whatever. With enough photos and impressions, he began erasing all traces of the footprints. He told the old men this was an official government investigation now. They were to keep their mouths shut, under penalty of law, or they would be arrested. Of course, this really pissed off the old men. Who did this man think he is? This was *their* project in the first place. Convinced now that this was alien activity, the old men didn't know exactly what to do.

Back on shore, the Montana man rented his own pontoon boat. He hired a company of tree cutters, took them back out to the island, and started cutting down the beech tree, loading the top part that had been burned and the hollow section just below onto his boat. He instructed the laborers to crate it up and ship it back to his lab in Montana. Watching from the shore, the old fishermen could see everything going on. They figured the aliens were coming up out of the lake, climbing to the top of the beech tree so their ship could pick them up. Maybe that's how the top of the tree got burned in the first place.

Fuming by this time, the fishermen were on more than a mission—they were going to demand to be kept informed. The Montana man firmly stated his position: they would be arrested if they interfered.

More than pissed off now, the fishermen decided to get their own proof of alien activity. The only person they could trust was Dick. He was, after all, a trustee in the resort's affairs. Dick was in his early fifties, young compared to the fishermen, who were in their early eighties. They were drinking buddies, after all. All the footprints on the island were gone. Could the prints from the original location still be there? It had not rained that much. The lake had gone down a couple of feet. With any luck, they could still be there.

Off to Dick's they went, making Dick swear he would not tell a soul what they were going to tell him. They decided to inform him only of the original footprint location, that's all. What they asked Dick to do was help them get imprints of some impressions in the mud along the lake. Not having any plaster, he decided to use his wife's candle, melting it down and filling in the impressions they wanted. Dick did not know where they were going or exactly what they wanted. Was he surprised when they lead him to the location where he tested his footprints! The prints were older, but they were still there, for the most part. With the seriousness of the old men at hand, Dick realized he must go along with whatever they wanted.

Slowly, Dick filled in a print with candle wax, using most of the candle. The old men were very pleased with the progress. A major problem was sand sticking to the wax. Back to Dick's they rushed with the completed impression. Dick could not help but sneak a laugh and grin every now and then. *What are these old men up to?* he thought. They could not possibly know he was the one who placed the footprints there. In Dick's kitchen, they put Dick in charge of cleaning up the footprint, arguing among themselves as to how it should be done. One of the men asked Dick if he believed in aliens. "No, not at all," stated Dick.

One of the old men told Dick he saw a UFO down at the lake about four weeks ago. It had red and green flashing lights and it was really big, about a hundred feet across. It had a glowing engine on the bottom. Dick by now realized what happened—the spaceship went out over the lake instead of up the hollow. This wax impression had to have something to do with it. Dick started asking if they found any other prints, wondering about the island prints, what the UFO looked like, and if anyone else had seen it. The old men clammed up after all the questioning. They thanked Dick and left, reminding him not to breathe a word of this to anyone.

Dick was about to burst, waiting for the next shift at work. He had to tell Art what had happened. The lake was infested with aliens, and UFOs were seen flying around. During the next three days, they figured everything out. The people in black and white must be alien hunters, probably government people. Dick decided to take a vacation and spend more time at the lake, which paid off handsomely. During the evening, around campfires and beer-drinking time, all the talk was about aliens. The Montana man must have changed his mind about the old fishermen and let them in on the scoop. He also sent them on a trip, maybe to keep them out of the way and quiet.

Chapter 6

Some of the nicest and most expensive motor homes you've ever seen started to enter the park. One of the motor homes parked right next to Dick's place. The best-looking woman he ever saw came stepping out, and right behind her what appeared to be her husband, both dressed in black. *Oh, no,* thought Dick, *they are on to me.*

Later that evening, around the campfire, the woman did get a little tipsy. While sitting next to Dick, she leaned over and whispered that they were really not married. They were on a special mission from headquarters, but she never elaborated what they were doing. She was all smiles, and her eyes were just glistening. Dick had never found himself in this position before, being married for thirty years; the thought had never crossed his mind before. He had to find out what they were doing there. He decided to do whatever was necessary for Art's and his protection.

Occupants of all the motor homes would walk around the park, making small talk with the full-time residents. Dick was not the least bit fooled by their actions; these people were government UFO hunters.

Back at work, Art and Dick decided to cool their heels for a while. Dick just listened to what everybody else had to say. Within a few days,

The Foot Brothers

the motor home next to Dick's found a place down the road where they could hook up. They must've thought this would give them a better overview of the entire resort. Dick had that woman on his mind now and those glistening eyes. Traveling around on his golf cart gave Dick the freedom he needed to get away. Art and Dick were concerned about the whereabouts of the old fishermen.

Working at night was not fun. Dick had the kind of job where he could go missing without anyone noticing. Art knew where he was going: to see the woman in the motor home, as they had planned it. Dick reported back about all the wonders in the motor home. It was full of electronic equipment, radar, satellite communications, closed-circuit television, and a remote-controlled helicopter. As it turns out, the man and woman could not stand each other. Taking turns at manning the radar station and all the other gear, one would go to the local hotel while the other worked.

This went on until the first of August. In the meantime, Dick got very good at flying the remote-controlled helicopter. Art got jealous of Dick, as it was always him who ended up with the women, but not this time. Coming back from their trip, the old fishermen would not discuss anything with Dick. Both boys wondered if they had a satellite parked overhead. Other black-and-whites—as they were being called—motored around the lake all day. What were they doing? Art decided to make a trip to the lake for firsthand information. Side-scan radar was the order of the day; that's what they were doing, checking the bottom of the lake. *Checking for what?* There was only thing they would be searching for— aliens. They thought aliens were living on the bottom of this lake, maybe in the sunken boats. Within a week, they had pulled out every boat that ever sank on the lake. By this time, Dick had gained the complete confidence of the woman. She even asked him if he wanted a job with them, even though she would never tell him exactly whom they worked for. Every now and then, she would mention that anyone trying to pull a hoax on them would face the wrath of the federal government.

Arthur Jude with Dick Hoy

Of course, the boys were very curious as to who was footing the bill for all this stuff. Hatching a plan to find out who was paying for all this and whom they worked for was easy. All they had to do was go through the garbage. On their next three days off, Dick would be visiting his—whatever you want to call her. Art was to get Grandpa's old truck, put his old Carhartts on, go unshaven, get really dirty, and go through her dumpster, pretending to be looking for aluminum cans.

The plan was perfect. About the edge of dark, Art arrived at the dumpster, jumped in, and started looking for paperwork. As he started to tear open paper sacks, a big rat went running across his head. All part of the job. Finished ripping the sack open, he found nothing but a used Kotex.

Just as Art was starting to get out, a siren started blowing. He thought he had better wait before he got out. He should have known—or Dick should have warned him—of the motion detectors on everything.

Inside the motor coach, the woman went into a rage, booted Dick out of the makeshift bed, and turned on the VCR that recorded all movement around the vehicle. She grabbed her pistol and intently watched the tape. Dick, somewhat startled also, realized what was happening and reassured her that it was just some old man looking for aluminum cans. "Why don't you just give me twenty dollars, and I will go out and give it to him to leave." Not wanting to get fully dressed, she agreed.

Dick did a fairly good job of directing the person in the dumpster out of the area and giving him the twenty dollars. She was watching everything on camera, so he had to do a good job.

After this, things seemed to change between them, and she would not invite him into the vehicle very often. Maybe she found out that Dick had met Art later that evening at the Buffalo Grill to drink up that twenty dollars.

The Foot Brothers

In late August, the boys really wanted to help their newfound friends obtain what they were looking for, aliens. Within a few days of discussing this at work, of course everyone at work wondered what they were talking about; they came up with a perfect plan. They would get an alien, sink her in the lake at the right time, turn her loose, and everyone would see her fly out of the lake. Simple. Maybe just maybe the black-and-whites would catch it on tape.

Art made another trip to downtown Columbus to Trader Buds. At the counter was one of the most beautiful women he had ever seen. She was purchasing St. Patrick's Day hats and horns, seventeen of each. *What an odd number*, thought Art, *and this time of year.* Art milled around the counter, hoping she would leave before he asked the sales clerk for a blow-up woman doll. She overheard anyway, and she just left laughing.

Back at the barn, the boys filled the doll full of helium and started painting her a purplish-brown color. Her skin, of course, was gray, with large black eyes. This is what an alien looks like, they reassured themselves. She was wearing a jumpsuit with some insignias on her upper arms, and she was set to go. Testing her in the water trough, they found it took eight cinder blocks to sink her. From Dick's days in Vietnam, they set about using the rattrap as the release mechanism for her. All one had to do was pull the trigger, and the razor blade fixed to the metal clamp would spring closed, cutting the small rope that held her down. It was as good as any claymore mine.

Back working nights now, the boys had no trouble staying awake all night on their days off. They had to make sure no one saw them. Where should they put her in the lake? It had to be by the bridge. Dick volunteered one more time go visit the woman in the motor coach. *Damn*, thought Art, *that ought to be me.* All was set. "Just make sure you keep her busy at three o' clock in the morning. I don't want her playing with her toys and catching me," Art demanded.

Arthur Jude with Dick Hoy

Alien woman

The Foot Brothers

Taking both fishing poles, Art set out on his mission; with the old rowboat in tow, he reached the lake with plenty of time. Keeping his alien sweetheart undercover, all he had to do was back the boat into the water and he was off. After fishing around the bridge for a short time, he tied one of the fishing pole's lines to the trigger mechanism on the rattrap and fed out enough line from the pole so the trigger wouldn't be pulled when she went overboard. There was a problem—how could he toss all the cinder blocks overboard at the same time? He lined all the blocks up along the edge of the boat. He had also measured just how much rope it would take for her to be underwater only a few inches with room for the rattrap. With a quickness he'd not had in years, Art threw all blocks overboard, which damn near turned the boat over. His only hope was that nobody saw him. Someone would think he was getting rid of a body. Slowly but surely, he paddled his way back to shore. By this time, it was five o' clock in the morning. Their plan was to meet back at Sharon's at six a.m. Both boys pulled into Sharon's driveway about the same time.

Sharon, always glad to see the boys, wondered what they'd been up to, arriving at this time of morning. "We're hungry, we've been fishing all night!", said Art then Dick.

Sure is strange, she thought, *fishing and not drinking?* You see, the boys never did any drinking while on a mission, only while they were planning a mission or working on one. She did make good sausage gravy, but not as good as Shirley's. Just before they were preparing to leave, Art asked Sharon—or more or less told her they had accidentally left Dick's fishing pole on the bank and asked if she would please go down and get it later that afternoon. It was in their favorite spot on the south shore, he affirmed.

"Sure," she responded. Not thinking any more about breakfast, she headed out about three o' clock. Finding the pole right away, she decided to do a little fishing of her own. She gave one good tug and then another, and it was caught on something. With all her might, she gave it one more powerful pull. Out flew the rattrap and all the excess line. She was bewildered at the trap flinging through air, wondering where it came from, but even more so at the angel dancing on top of the water about fifty yards from shore.

August afternoons are hot in southern Ohio. It did not take long for the alien, now angel, to warm up and fly off toward heaven. Knowing the boys had gotten her in the middle of something, she threw the fishing pole and rattrap in the back of her pickup, and down the road she went.

Later that evening, a county sheriff from the next county showed up at her door. He is the illegitimate offspring of her Dad's brother Doug. They knew each other, but not very well. He just wanted to know if she had been down at the lake that afternoon. "Well, yes, I was. I went down to do a little fishing, but I started feeling bad, so I just left. Why do you want to know?"

"Did you see anything strange or out of place?" the sheriff asked.

"This medicine I take gives me blurred vision and makes me sick sometimes. No, I did not see anything," Sharon replied.

With that information, he left, appearing well satisfied. She went straight to the mantel and placed the photo of the boys on her bosom, giving them a big hug. Not knowing what the boys were up to did not matter. She was in the middle of it, and that was all that counted.

Chapter 7

The following few weeks seemed like an eternity; their turns at work just dragged by. Dick spent all of his days off at the lake, even taking a day off from work. He heard absolutely nothing from anyone; even the old fishermen had nothing to say. His woman would barely speak to him now.

Labor Day was coming up, and Art planned on spending time at the lake with Dick. Maybe both of them could break the silence. Arriving at the lake, the boys could not believe their eyes. Someone had cut down or more or less ripped out all of the pine forest. It was terrible—all those big, beautiful pine trees gone; their launch pad gone; and the shade along the road all gone. The only thing left was an old, dead stump of a beech tree right in the middle of what used to be a beautiful forest. Art recalled Grandpa telling him that he helped plant those pines when he was a young man working for the CCC.

Art and Dick vowed revenge but still heard nothing.

Putting their thinking caps on, they hatched a plan to have the aliens cook up a feast. (Everybody knows aliens love a good barbecue). With all the black-and-whites walking around, one of them would have to find their cookout spot sooner or later.

What would the boys need for it to look like an alien barbecue spot? Bones, all kinds of bones—catfish bones, deer bones, turtle bones, turkey bones, dog bones, cat bones, snake bones, and most of all, human bones. All of which, except the last, were easily found around the lake. Dick was to obtain all the bones except the human ones, which was Art's job. Art was to also make something that would leave bite marks on the bones. That was easy: getting some different-size hacksaw blades, heating them up so they could form a semicircle, using several sizes. Now to the human bones.

Hospital or graveyard, it had to be one or the other. How? *Nurses*, thought Art, *I will start hanging out in the bars close to hospitals. There I can get close to a nurse. She will get me my bones—a toe, a finger, anything.* After finding out when payday was for the nurses, Art was busy in the bar. He needed a surgical nurse to get her hands on bones, so Art screened them carefully. He was not as smooth as he used to be, but he could handle his own. He found three sitting together, one of them rather large. He proceeded to buy them a round of beers, and they, of course, welcomed him over. The only surgical nurse there was the big one. He launched his plan to have this woman help him obtain bones. One of the better-looking women listening to Art's line spouted out, "Who are you, Jeffrey Dahmer? Get the hell out of here, you pervert," and threw a beer on him. Art left the bar in a hurry with beer cans flying at him. *Well, that did not work*, he reckoned.

"We are going to have to dig up a grave," he told Dick. Dick had always been leery of ghosts and spirits; sometimes Art thought Dick really believed in them. "I know where a perfect grave is that we can dig up and nobody will ever know. Down by the water-treatment plant, there is a graveyard that was closed to new graves in 1935. Nobody ever goes there, so nobody will ever know. It's right by the water's edge. On a moonless night, all we have to do is paddle across the lake and dig up the bones. We will only take a few rib bones anyway, cover it back up, and we are out of there. Besides, the grave I'm talking about has been there since 1898. He won't care."

Dick was very apprehensive about this whole deal.

"After what I have done for you these last couple of months, you ought to be glad to do this," said Art.

Dick reluctantly agreed. Art had a better understanding of Dick's beliefs in ghosts and spirits. This would be a good time to pay him back for the dumpster affair.

It was Art's idea to do this, and Dick was a reluctant participant. *Perfect*, thought Art, *I can pay him back, and he will never be the wiser.* Looking through his storage boxes, Art found a micro-miniature tape recorder. He installed new batteries, and with a new tape, Art began the verbiage of what a person buried for over one hundred years would say. "What are you doing? Get out of my grave! What are you doing? Get out of my grave!" in a different tone, over and over. The recorder could just be left in the grave.

They checked the *Farmer's Almanac*, and the second week in September seemed perfect for this to go on. Both donned their old Carhartts and headed for the location across the lake. You could barely see your hand in front of your face. Making it safely to the other shore with shovels in hand, they ran into a large thorn patch. No way could they get through here; they had to walk around it. Finally at the graveyard, Dick started to shake a little. Both started digging, and within a few feet, they hit top boards. "Here," said Art, "let me finish it." Art burst through sideboards with his shovel, and Dick got farther away. It was the perfect opportunity for Art to reach into his front pocket and pull out the recorder. Placing it in the coffin, he pulled out a dried-up rib bone. "One more," said Art. With the recorder, he reached in and pressed the button. "What are you doing? Get out of my grave!" Dick was beside himself. "Did you hear that? Did you hear that?" he asked in a voice Art had never heard before out of Dick.

"I don't hear anything. Be quiet." Art leaned back over, getting one more rib bone, and Dick took off running as fast as he could go, straight through the thorn patch. Art refilled the grave and made his way around to the boat with both ribs. Dick's face looked like five pounds of hamburger; there was not a place on him that was not scratched from the thorns. "Man, you look bad. What the hell is the matter with you?" asked Art.

"You tell me you did not hear that!" said Dick.

"No, I did not hear anything. Get a hold of yourself," said Art.

Back across the lake they went and on to Sharon's to doctor Dick up. While in their secret room, taking care of Dick, Art forgot about the tape recorder. He meant to leave it in the grave. Instead he stuck it in his back pocket, the one with the hole in it. Why it had to fall out there, no

The Foot Brothers

one knows, but it did, hitting the floor and turning itself on. "What are you doing? Get out of my grave!" They just looked at each other, and Art started laughing. Fire flew out of Dick's eyes, the only place on him that wasn't already blood red.

Dick hit Art so hard, it knocked him through the wall and into the pigpen outside. With the wall busted into several pieces, Dick grabbed a two-by-four to finish Art off. Hearing Art outside hollering for help, Dick knew he had him licked for sure. Dick jumped through the hole in the wall and landed knee deep in pig shit and mud. Looking around for Art to finish him off, Dick saw the most God-awful thing you could ever see. Art had landed on the feed trough, face down. Art's prize boar hog, weighing five hundred pounds, was "porking" Art squarely in the rear. Art was hollering, "Get him off me, get him off me, help, help!" It looked like that boar was trying to chew on Art's ear. If it had not been for the Carhartt hood still being in good shape, Art's ear would be gone. A little bit of *Deliverance* here, but it's true. Dick was laughing so hard, he couldn't stand up; it's hard to walk in this stuff anyway. What could he do? What could anyone possibly do with a five-hundred-pound boar hog intent on spreading his seed?

Slowly making his way to Art, Dick figured on the only thing that might save Art. He hauled off with the two-by-four and smacked the boar as hard as he could in the nuts, breaking the two-by-four in two. He did have a big target. The boar let out a loud squeal and ran to the other side of the pigpen. Dick helped Art back through the hole and out of the pen. Dick was still laughing when he was not struggling with Art. Back inside, they both composed themselves, Art swore he was going to shoot that hog right now. Dick was still laughing. Art said he was going to tie that hog in the barn and burn the barn down around it. Dick was still laughing. Art knew he had to do something or he would be the laughing stock of the county. Dick was still laughing. "Look," said Art, "if you don't ever tell anyone about this, I won't mention the grave digging."

"Agreed," said Dick. With that settled, they went outside to clean up. I don't know if you ever had pig shit on you, but it's impossible to clean off with one washing.

Sharon was awakened by all the commotion and noise. She leaned out the window to find out what was going on and was told that everything was all right. Art yelled, "Saturday the slaughterhouse will be coming to take the boar."

Early the next morning, Art called the slaughterhouse and told the man he wanted the boar completely ground up into sausage.

"Don't do that. Why don't you at least make some pork chops and some smoked ham?"

"Well, OK," said Art. "Deliver it out to Sharon's when you get done." Art was out of the prize pig business. "No wonder I never had won any prizes with that SOB," Art goes off a mumbling about some damn queer hog.

Within a week, four hundred pounds of pork was delivered to Sharon's. She had no place to put it all. She had thirty pounds of sausage she had to find a place for. Getting close to Sunday, she informed her church and all the family that she would be cooking breakfast for everyone after services. They all showed up, even Art. Art refused to eat any sausage; no one figured out why. "Feed it to the dogs," he said.

Dick's face had cleared up, and Art's ribs and back were a little bit achy. Never mind the rest of him. Back to the bones: putting all of the animal bones in a large pot and boiling them for several hours seemed to do the trick. Teeth made out of hacksaw blades would make an impression on just about anything. The rib bones were too delicate for boiling; however, they did take a good gnawing from the teeth. Gnawing from the ribs was dumped in the pot with the rest of the bones.

Where would aliens have a barbecue? On top of a ridge or on the beach somewhere? Neither; they would have it on one of the houseboats parked in the marina. Parking their pontoon boat in the marina for a week gave them plenty of time and opportunity to plant a barbecue site on one of the larger boats. That way someone was sure to find it. With the pile of bones they left behind, the owner must call the police. Not only would the pile of bones signal some type of intrusion, but the boys brought with them a bucket of mud and dipped the alien foot impressions into the mud and placed them all over everything. The owner of this boat was going to be someone special.

"Do aliens eat humans?" Art asked Dick.

"I guess they do. They eat everything else."

"The last one of their barbecues I went to, they had some human ribs with Jack Daniel's barbecue sauce."

"Well, in that case, my old lady best straighten up, or she is going to be feed for the aliens." Both boys had a good laugh.

Chapter 8

Waiting to hear something about anything kept the boys wondering what the black-and-whites were up to. They saw them all around the park, but no one was talking, nothing.

"We have to do something. We need to get them back out in the open," said Art.

"You know," recalled Dick, "last summer, she mentioned that they think aliens are coming to Earth to have their little ones."

"Well, maybe they are. What can we do to help them find out?" said Art.

"I don't know. She mentioned something about eggs, finding their eggs or something."

"What kind of eggs?" said Art.

"I guess like a chicken egg, but larger. You know aliens weigh about forty-five pounds when they are grown. So they would have to be about ten times the size of a chicken egg," said Dick.

"How in the hell can I make an egg?" asked Art. "What does an alien egg look like?"

"I don't know," said Dick, "but work on it."

The Foot Brothers

Returning home from work, Art walked into the middle of a water-balloon fight between the neighborhood boys. One hit him right on top of his balding head, getting water all over him. He turned to chase them away and was smacked once more. Still undaunted, he started after them and was smacked once more. The fourth water balloon was headed right for him. He caught it before it exploded. Art held the balloon by its end, ready to return fire.

Stranger things have happened. Holding the balloon by its tail, Art realized it was about ten times the size of a chicken egg. If someone used their imagination, this could be a perfect model alien egg. Pelted three or four more times, Art was soaked before he got into his house.

Art hung the balloon in the freezer by clamping a popsicle stick he had stuck inside, so the embryo could harden up. He set about finding something he could dip the balloon in, just like a Dairy Queen treat, all covered in chocolate. But this would be covered in alien eggshell, whatever that is.

It was the first week of October, and the boys knew they did not have time to spare before cold weather set in. One thing Art knew he needed was eggshells, plenty of them. This was the time of year for Sharon to start making her pickled eggs, just like Grandma, for next year's fair. Art loved pickled eggs. He would sometimes help Grandma make hers. Showing up at Sharon's the next day with ten dozen eggs was not out of place. Even Dick showed up later. They worked all morning, boiling and peeling eggs. Sharon never thought anything of Art putting the shells in a separate bag instead of the trash. She thought this would be a good time to find out all she could about last summer and the fishing pole incident.

"Do you boys believe in aliens?" she asked. "'Cause I thought I seen something last summer. There has been a lot of talk about them at the church and down at the lake."

Art said, "You have been taking too much medication. Do you understand what it would take for a UFO or alien to come here? It's millions and millions of miles to the closest place a human or anything like us might live. Have you ever heard of SETI? These are the people that send out the most powerful radio signals we have. After their signals travel about one light year away, they decay into space electrical noise, no good for anything. People out on the ocean at night report seeing UFOs in the water. That's just a small type of krill that when distributed emits light. If people want to see something, they will see it. If people want to believe there are aliens here on Earth, then there will be aliens here."

"Well, OK," said Sharon. She was hanging her head when telling the boys that she had to send her old horse off to the glue factory.

With all the eggs taken care of and ready for pickling, Art said the rest of the work was woman's work and he was leaving. That's the way Grandma and he always did it. Grandma never told him she pickled her eggs in Jack Daniel's.

Taking the eggshells with them out on the steps, Art jumped for glory. "I got it," he said, "bone glue."

"What in the hell are you talking about?" Dick wanted to know.

Back at Art's, the boys baked the eggshells good and dry. Getting out the blender, they commenced to grind the eggshells into a powder so fine, it escaped on its own around the top of the blender. When placed on the counter, it started dispersing on its own. "I bet the government would like to know about that," said Art.

"Be careful with that stuff. It might cause us to grow feathers," said Dick.

Satisfied with enough eggshell powder, they awaited the arrival of the bone glue Art ordered. Art could not wait for Dick's assistance in cooking the bone glue on the stove. It stank so badly, it ran him out of the house. It's a good thing Shirley was not home. Off to the barn and secret room they went.

Using the water from boiling the bones, slowly mixing in the bone glue, then the eggshell powder, they had one of the stinkiest concoctions you ever smelled. Art had to run back home to obtain the frozen water

The Foot Brothers

balloons. He found Dick outside. He could not take the smell. They decided to go to the factory and borrow rubber gloves and breathing respirators. They watched the temperature of the concoction closely, as they had asked the Dairy Queen manager what temperature he kept his chocolate.

They slowly dipped the balloons into the concoction. They began to be covered with a shell, a very thick, light-brown shell with white specks all throughout. It hardened up rather quickly because of the ice inside. The boys clamped the eggs using the popsicle stick in the vise and poured the remaining concoction on top. As the ice was starting to melt, the concoction firmed up quite nicely. The boys looked like two mad scientists. When a lot of water started pouring out of the first egg, it was removed from the vise. Art held the egg, and Dick pulled out the mostly melted water balloon, shouting, "It's alive! It's alive!" The bottom of the egg split in several places.

"I guess that's normal when they hatch out," said Art. They put the egg in the cooler, celebrating the birth of their first alien baby with a beer or ten. Several more were made, but the first is always the most special.

Working three days on, three days off gave the boys ample time for performing all that was necessary. Most of the planning was done at work. Their biggest problem now was how to have the black-and-whites find the birthplace of the baby and its empty eggshell. Dick set out to make some baby footprints with eight-inch rebar. Perfect prints were in hand.

Where to have the birth? A cave, no. Under a bridge, no. In a barn, a manger; forgive them, but where else could it be? Old man Lee's—he always goes to Florida the first of September. They could sneak in his barn and leave the egg, have one set of large footprints going in and one set of large footprints plus one set of really small footprints coming out. What else could anyone think? But how to make sure they are found?

Barn where Alien egg was placed

The Foot Brothers

Art decided that if they had all that electronic stuff in the motor lab, they must have telemetry radio-signal tracking equipment. Dick responded, "I think she does." With that information, Art built two radio-transmitting units, nothing special, but powered by a car battery, they could transmit halfway across the Earth. This was the type kids used to build for Morse code training forty years ago. The key or encoding mechanism was out of this world. It consisted of a wheel with binary codes cut into the outer ring; both rings were identical. The wheel operated a switch that caused the transmitter to transmit. It could be turned 360 degrees in both directions. The codes did not spell out anything, but someone surely will come up with a message contained in the code. They devised a method of operating both transmitters at their specific time and place. Dick volunteered to transmit from the barn; if they came looking too quickly, he knew the back roads and probably could get away. Art was to drive to the next-biggest lake, about twenty miles away, and transmit.

Radio Transmitters

Arthur Jude with Dick Hoy

Meeting in Cambridge, the boys set their clocks together. They had also purchased two birthday balloons from the grocery store and tied some aluminum foil to each, so the radar could pick them up. They were to be set off five miles in the opposite direction. If they were manning the radar, the black-and-whites would be going in the wrong direction. Art set his balloon off at the edge of the next lake; watching it, he understood what had happened to their spaceship. This balloon traveled across the lake about twenty feet above the water in a straight line until it was out of sight. At exactly ten thirty, Dick set his transmitter off, and at exactly ten thirty-five Art set his transmitter off. Then waiting five minutes, both transmitted for five minutes. Dick could not finish his second transmission. He saw lights coming. Wisely, he got the hell out of there.

Art was late getting back to Cambridge; he was to transmit all the way down to Cambridge in case they were getting close to Dick.

Dick was scared, shaking at the thought that he was caught. The boys had a stiff drink and went home. The next day, Dick planned on being back at the lake to watch for any signs of activity.

Activity was not the word for it. There must have been fifty people at Old Man Lee's barn. They were crisscrossing his pasture on a precise grid, all with their heads down, looking for something. Even the county sheriff showed up. In the distance, Dick could see his woman there. The next day was Saturday, and there was always a party at the clubhouse. He was sure she would be there.

All smiles, she was there, really dressed up. She informed Dick she had found what she was looking for. She would be going to Washington for a while but would be back. Only a skeleton crew would stay.

This time of year, the lake resort started shutting down. All the old folks went to Florida, and very few people stayed all winter. The rest of November the boys spent laughing, waiting on the Christmas party, when they felt for sure she would be back. At work, everybody wondered what they were up to. Dick had gone to the lake to winterize his place, and she

The Foot Brothers

was there. This was right before Christmas. She mentioned a big pay raise and promotion was coming her way. If Dick still wanted a job, she could arrange it. They could meet later if Dick cared to.

All of December, the boys laughed. They had never had so much fun, wondering where their egg went. To this day, they still don't know. They might as well put up a sign letting the whole world know when the aliens will be back. Art had stolen a highway sign from Indiana or Illinois while on his travels: Pink Stuff Road. You can't blame a fellow for stealing a sign like that. On the back of it, they used hieroglyphics to write.

It's still nailed to the old beech tree stump in the middle of what used to be a pine forest.

Chapter 9

I don't know if this is true or not, they did tell me this, but you decide if you believe it.

By the middle of February, the boys were out of their minds with boredom and pissed off at the fact that everybody else was making a lot of money from what they had accomplished. Even the old fishermen had come into some money. They had fixed up their places and gone to Florida for the winter. The boys, on the other hand, had spent over three hundred bucks on the spaceship, truck rental, blow-up woman—which seemed like the only type Art could catch anymore—reflective paint, eggs, rebar. You can't count the beer.

With only a skeleton crew left, what could the boys possibly do to them? "Abduct them," said Dick.

"How in the hell can we do that?" asked Art.

"Simple. We will learn hypnotism. We will practice on each other."

"No you won't, not on me anyway," responded Art. "I know. I will get a couple Tyvek work suits from work and paint them up like we did our ladies. You put it on. You will make one of the best aliens a person could hope for. All you have to do is run across their parking lot, in front of the camera. I will be waiting for you in the truck at the bend."

Buffallo Grill. Was burnt down

"Oh, no, you will get me shot," said Dick. "How is that going to abduct them?"

A few days later, they came up with a plan. The two on the skeleton crew went to the Buffalo Grill every Sunday night and got totally soused. The owner of the grill knew the boys quite well. Art asked him if he needed extra help on Sunday. Art would work all day. That way the owner could have a day off. He was glad to get out of there. This normally would make Art's wife mad, but they needed the money. She wanted him out of the house on those winter days; all they did was argue.

Once someone is abducted, where are they taken? To the spaceship, of course. How do they remember what happened to them? What does happen?

Recalling all the news accounts of people being abducted, the boys set about remodeling the back end of another U-Haul truck. This one had a passage from the cab into the box on back. They lined the walls and roof with aluminum foil, painted insignias all over everything, and built two small beds (operating tables), with plenty of bright lights. They ended up with a perfect interior of a spaceship operating room, and the boys were well satisfied.

If you ever had to walk a drunk to their car, you know it is rather difficult. How to get them from the bar into the back of the spaceship? The Buffalo Grill was not very busy on Sunday night; Art could close up anytime he wanted, or when there were no customers. The two skeleton-crew members showed up as usual on that cold, rainy March night. Art called Dick to bring the truck and park it out back. The game was on. Their plans did require the boys to don the Tyvek suits they had painted. Dick had painted his as though he was a superhero. Art was the head doctor, all white with special insignias.

Working there almost a month, having them as customers every Sunday, they got to know each other. Both thought Art was a real loser, as they had one of the most important jobs one could have. Art was just a lousy bartender. About eleven o' clock, Art noticed through the front window the headlights of their truck driving around back. He told his two customers that he was closing up, but he wanted them to stay and do a little free drinking with him. They were glad to; nothing but top shelf. Art controlled his drinking and plied them with all the free drinks they could handle. As a matter of fact, Art had switched to straight Coke, while they were on straight Jack Daniel's. By twelve o' clock, they were passed out on the bar.

Art headed for the back door to inform Dick of the consequences. They both donned their alien suits and masks. The two customers were so drunk, both boys had to help each one of them to the back of the spaceship, taking more time than they wanted. But they got them there. The ship was filled with five or six alien nurses the boys had painted up. Most were tied to the floor, but two were allowed to float to the top of the truck. Laying them each on their tables, the bright lights were turned on.

The Foot Brothers

The woman had the biggest tits Dick had ever seen; they each would fill a five-gallon bucket. He had to squeeze them at least once. Getting on his knees, he scooted over next to the boobs and gave them a good massage. About this time, Art came through the front hatch door with a kid's toy microphone, saying, "Bring in the inseminator. Bring in the inseminator." Dick made his way around to the back of the spaceship truck. Standing up, he grabbed the broom they had left for this purpose and poked the guy squarely in the ass. "Abort mission. Abort mission," was the command heard from Art. "You have inseminated the wrong one; you have inseminated the wrong one."

With this, the lights went out. The boys helped them to their car, and Art went back in and finished closing up. Down the road they went, leaving the two to sober up. The two skeleton-crew members did finally wake up, recalling some if not all of what happened. They were reluctant to check with headquarters. When they did, they were very vague. Headquarters decided to send in Axle to check up on them. He was their troubleshooter. Arriving at the motor lab, he found them sitting around, with the place in a mess. The woman was eating take-out Chinese with her newfound best friend, a woman. Axle asked the man to straighten up the place and pick the typewriter up off the floor. He said he couldn't; he shouldn't pick anything up because he was pregnant.

Axle called headquarters and informed his boss that one of them was pregnant and the other turned queer. "That's too bad about her being pregnant. She could suck the eye out of a tornado," his boss responded. "The guy we don't care."

"You don't understand. The guy thinks he is pregnant, and the girl turned," Axle explained.

"Shut that operation down, and get them out of there."

This is a true story. The names have been changed to protect the guilty.

> There is no such thing as Bigfoot.
> There is no such thing as the Mothman.
> And if there are aliens out there, God would not let them come to this Earth.

Made in the USA
Middletown, DE
30 March 2022